ParaPro Assessment Study Guide
Test Prep Secrets for the Paraprofessional Exam

Table of Contents

Introduction

The fact that you've purchased this book means two things. The first: You're preparing for, or at least considering, the ParaPro exam. The second: You've already made an excellent first step in picking up this study guide.

We'll provide you with a detailed overview of the ParaPro, so that you know exactly what to expect on test day. We'll also cover all of the subjects over which you will be tested, as well as provide multiple practice sections for you to test your knowledge and improve. No worries – even if it's been a while since your last major examination, we'll make sure you're more than ready!

What is the ParaPro?

The ParaPro exam developed by ETS to measure the skills of reading, writing, and math for prospective and practicing paraprofessionals in response to the federal legislation known as the No Child Left Behind Act. Along with holding an associates of the arts degree (or 2 years of college courses completed), passing the ParaPro Assessment is a requirement for anyone wanting to instruct children in the classroom.

Breaking Down the ParaPro Assesment Exam

You will have 2.5 hours to complete all sections of the test of which there are a total of 90 questions. Those sections are:

- **Writing**
  - 30 Questions: Tests knowledge of vocabulary, grammar and usage.

- **Math**
  - 30 Questions: Tests knowledge of math (pre-algebra, algebra, geometry, etc.)

- **Reading**
  - 30 Questions: Tests reading comprehension through questions over multiple passages.

Scoring

The makers of the test do not set a qualifying or passing score. Instead, each state or district sets their own requirements for minimum standards, so it is important to check with the school district of where you plan to teach.

How This Book Works

The subsequent chapters in this book are divided into a review of those topics covered on the exam. This is not to "teach" or "re-teach" you these concepts – there is no way to cram all of that material into one book! Instead, we are going to help you recall all of the information which you've already learned. Even more importantly, we'll show you how to apply that knowledge.

Each chapter includes an extensive review, with practice drills at the end to test your knowledge. With time, practice, and determination, you'll be well-prepared for test day.

Chapter 1: The Writing Section

The first step in getting ready for this section of the test consists of reviewing the basic techniques used to determine the meanings of words you are not familiar with. The good news is that you have been using various degrees of these techniques since you first began to speak. Sharpening these skills will also help you with this subtest.

Following each section you will find a practice drill. Use your score on these to determine if you need to study that particular subject matter further. At the end of the chapter you will find a review of the concepts and a chapter test. The questions found on the practice drills and chapter test are not given in the two formats found on the English subtest; rather they are designed to reinforce the skills needed to score well on the English subtest.

VOCABULARY and GRAMMAR

It's time to review those basic techniques used to determine the meanings of words with which you are not familiar. Don't worry though! The good news is that you have been using various degrees of these techniques since you first began to speak.

We have not included a vocabulary list in this book, because reading definitions from a page is the worst way to improve word knowledge. Interaction, and seeing the words used in context, is the best way to learn. We recommend using flashcards to improve your vocabulary knowledge – there are many resources available online. The best we've found is www.vocabulary.com/il; but you should find what suits you specifically!

Below are techniques for improving and utilizing the vocabulary you already have.

Context Clues

The most fundamental vocabulary skill is using the context of a word to determine its meaning. Your ability to observe sentences closely is extremely useful when it comes to understanding new vocabulary words.

Types of Context
There are two different types of context that can help you understand the meaning of unfamiliar words: **sentence context** and **situational context**. Regardless of which context is present, these types of questions are not really testing your knowledge of vocabulary; rather, they test your ability to comprehend the meaning of a word through its usage.

Situational context is context that comes from understanding the situation in which a word or phrase occurs.

Sentence context occurs within the sentence that contains the vocabulary word. To figure out words using sentence context clues, you should first determine the most important words in the sentence.

Example: I had a hard time reading her <u>illegible</u> handwriting.
   a) Neat.
   b) Unsafe.
   c) Sloppy.
   d) Educated.

Already, you know that this sentence is discussing something that is hard to read. Look at the word that **illegible** is describing: **handwriting**. Based on context clues, you can tell that illegible means that her handwriting is hard to read.

Next, look at the answer choices. Choice **a) Neat** is obviously a wrong answer because neat handwriting would not be difficult to read. Choice **b) Unsafe** and **d) Educated** don't make sense. Therefore, choice **c) Sloppy** is the best answer choice.

of Clues
re four types of clues that can help you understand context, and therefore the meaning of a word. **restatement**, **positive/negative**, **contrast**, and **specific detail**.

tatement clues occur when the definition of the word is clearly stated in the sentence.

Example: The dog was <u>dauntless</u> in the face of danger, braving the fire to save the girl.
   a) Difficult.
   b) Fearless.
   c) Imaginative.

nstrating **bravery** in the face of danger would be **fearless,** choice **b)**. In this case,
text clues tell you exactly what the word means.

8

Positive/negative clues can tell you whether a word has a positive or negative meaning.

> **Example**: The magazine gave a great review of the fashion show, stating the clothing was **sublime**.
> a) Horrible.
> b) Exotic.
> c) Bland
> d) Gorgeous.

The sentence tells us that the author liked the clothing enough to write a **great** review, so you know that the best answer choice is going to be a positive word. Therefore, you can immediately rule out choices **a)** and **c)** because they are negative words. **Exotic** is a neutral word; alone, it doesn't inspire a **great** review. The most positive word is gorgeous, which makes choice **d) Gorgeous** the best answer.

The following sentence uses both restatement and positive/negative clues:

> "Janet suddenly found herself destitute, so poor she could barely afford to eat."

The second part of the sentence clearly indicates that destitute is a negative word; it also restates the meaning: very poor.

Contrast clues include the opposite meaning of a word. Words like **but**, **on the other hand**, and **however** are tip-offs that a sentence contains a contrast clue.

> **Example**: Beth did not spend any time preparing for the test, but Tyron kept a rigorous study schedule.
> a) Strict.
> b) Loose.
> c) Boring.
> d) Strange.

In this case, the word **but** tells us that Tyron studied in a different way than Beth. If Beth did not study very hard, then Tyron did study hard for the test. The best answer here, therefore, is choice **a) Strict**.

Specific detail clues give a precise detail that can help you understand the meaning of the word.

> **Example**: The box was heavier than he expected and it began to become cumbersome.
> a) Impossible.
> b) Burdensome.
> c) Obligated.
> d) Easier.

Start by looking at the specific details of the sentence. Choice **d)** can be eliminated right because it is doubtful it would become **easier** to carry something that is **heavier**. There are no clues in the sentence to indicate he was **obligated** to carry the box, so choice **c)** can a disregarded. The sentence specifics, however, do tell you that the package was cumbe

9

because it was heavy to carry; something heavy to carry is a burden, which is **burdensome**, choice **b)**.

It is important to remember that more than one of these clues can be present in the same sentence. The more there are, the easier it will be to determine the meaning of the word, so look for them.

Denotation and Connotation

As you know, many English words have more than one meaning. For example, the word **quack** has two distinct definitions: the sound a duck makes; and a person who publicly pretends to have a skill, knowledge, education, or qualification which they do not possess.

The **denotations** of a word are the dictionary definitions.

The **connotations** of a word are the implied meaning(s) or emotion which the word makes you think.

> **Example**: "Sure," Pam said excitedly, "I'd just love to join your club; it sounds so exciting!"

> Now, read this sentence:

> "Sure," Pam said sarcastically, "I'd just love to join your club; it sounds so exciting!"

Even though the two sentences only differ by one word, they have completely different meanings. The difference, of course, lies in the words "excitedly" and "sarcastically."

away
also
so be
rsome

Nouns, Pronouns, Verbs, Adjectives, and Adverbs

Nouns
Nouns are people, places, or things. They are typically the subject of a sentence. For example, "The hospital was very clean." The noun is "hospital;" it is the "place."

Pronouns
Pronouns essentially "replace" nouns. This allows a sentence to not sound repetitive. Take the sentence: "Sam stayed home from school because Sam was not feeling well." The word "Sam" appears twice in the same sentence. Instead, you can use a pronoun and say, "Sam stayed at home because *he* did not feel well." Sounds much better, right?

Most Common Pronouns:

- I, me, mine, my.

- You, your, yours.

- He, him, his.

- She, her, hers.

- It, its.

- We, us, our, ours.

- They, them, their, theirs.

Verbs
Remember the old commercial, "Verb: It's what you do"? That sums up verbs in a nutshell! Verbs are the "action" of a sentence; verbs "do" things.

They can, however, be quite tricky. Depending on the subject of a sentence, the tense of the word (past, present, future, etc.), and whether or not they are regular or irregular, verbs have many variations.

Example: "He runs to second base." The verb is "runs." This is a "regular verb."

Example: "I am 7 years old." The verb in this case is "am." This is an "irregular verb."

As mentioned, verbs must use the correct tense – and that tense must remain the same throughout the sentence. "I was baking cookies and eat some dough." That sounded strange, didn't it? That's because the two verbs "baking" and "eat" are presented in different tenses. "Was baking" occurred in the past; "eat," on the other hand, occurs in the present. Instead, it should be "**ate** some dough."

Adjectives
Adjectives are words that describe a noun and give more information. Take the sentence: "The boy hit the ball." If you want to know more about the noun "boy," then you could use an adjective to describe it.

"The **little** boy hit the ball." An adjective simply provides more information about a noun or subject in a sentence.

Adverb

For some reason, many people have a difficult time with adverbs – but don't worry! They are really quite simple. Adverbs are similar to adjectives in that they provide more information; however, they describe verbs, adjectives, and even other adverbs. They do **not** describe nouns – that's an adjective's job.

Take the sentence: "The doctor said she hired a new employee."

It would give more information to say: "The doctor said she **recently** hired a new employee." Now we know more about *how* the action was executed. Adverbs typically describe when or how something has happened, how it looks, how it feels, etc.

Good vs. Well
A very common mistake that people make concerning adverbs is the misuse of the word "good."

"Good" is an adjective – things taste good, look good, and smell good. "Good" can even be a noun – "Superman does good" – when the word is speaking about "good" vs. "evil." HOWEVER, "good" is never an adverb.

People commonly say things like, "I did really good on that test," or, "I'm good." Ugh! This is NOT the correct way to speak! In those sentences, the word "good" is being used to describe an action: how a person **did**, or how a person **is**. Therefore, the adverb "well" should be used. "I did really **well** on that test." "I'm **well**."

The correct use of "well" and "good" can make or break a person's impression of your grammar – make sure to always speak correctly!

The Parts of Words

Although you are not expected to know every word in the English language for your test, you will need to have the ability to use deductive reasoning to find the choice that is the best match for the word in question, which is why we are going to explain how to break a word into its parts of meaning

prefix – root – suffix

One trick in dividing a word into its parts is to first divide the word into its **syllables**. To show how syllables can help you find roots and affixes, we'll use the word **descendant,** which means one who comes from an ancestor. Start by dividing the word into its individual syllables; this word has three: **de-scend-ant**. The next step is to look at the beginning and end of the word, and then determine if these syllables are prefixes, suffixes, or possible roots. You can then use the meanings of each part to guide you in defining the word. When you divide words into their specific parts, they do not always add up to an exact definition, but you will see a relationship between their parts.

> **Note:** This trick won't always work in every situation, because not all prefixes, roots, and suffixes have only one syllable. For example, take the word **monosyllabic** (which ironically means "one syllable"). There are five syllables in that word, but only three parts. The prefix is "mono," meaning "one." The root "syllab" refers to "syllable," while the suffix "ic" means

"pertaining to." Therefore, we have one very long word which means "pertaining to one syllable."

The more familiar you become with these fundamental word parts, the easier it will be to define unfamiliar words. Although the words found on the Word Knowledge subtest are considered vocabulary words learned by the tenth grade level of high school, some are still less likely to be found in an individual's everyday vocabulary. The root and affixes list in this chapter uses more common words as examples to help you learn them more easily. Don't forget that you use word roots and affixes every day, without even realizing it. Don't feel intimidated by the long list of roots and affixes (prefixes and suffixes) at the end of this chapter, because you already know and use them every time you communicate with some else, verbally and in writing. If you take the time to read through the list just once a day for two weeks, you will be able to retain most of them and understand a high number of initially unfamiliar words.

Roots, Prefixes, and Suffixes

Roots
Roots are the building blocks of all words. Every word is either a root itself or has a root. Just as a plant cannot grow without roots, neither can vocabulary, because a word must have a root to give it meaning.

      Example: The test instructions were **unclear.**

The root is what is left when you strip away all the prefixes and suffixes from a word. In this case, take away the prefix "un-," and you have the root **clear.**

Roots are not always recognizable words, because they generally come from Latin or Greek words, such as **nat**, a Latin root meaning **born**. The word native, which means a person born of a referenced placed, comes from this root, so does the word prenatal, meaning before birth. Yet, if you used the prefix **nat** instead of born, just on its own, no one would know what you were talking about.
Words can also have more than one root. For example, the word **omnipotent** means all powerful. Omnipotent is a combination of the roots **omni-**, meaning all or every, and **-potent**, meaning power or strength. In this case, **omni** cannot be used on its own as a single word, but **potent** can.

Again, it is important to keep in mind that roots do not always match the exact definitions of words and they can have several different spellings, but breaking a word into its parts is still one of the best ways to determine its meaning.

Prefixes

Prefixes are syllables added to the beginning of a word and suffixes are syllables added to the end of the word. Both carry assigned meanings. The common name for prefixes and suffixes is **affixes**. Affixes do not have to be attached directly to a root and a word can often have more than one prefix and/or suffix. Prefixes and suffixes can be attached to a word to completely change the word's meaning or to enhance the word's original meaning. Although they don't mean much to us on their own, when attached to other words affixes can make a world of difference.

Let's use the word **prefix** itself as an example:

Fix means to place something securely.

Pre means before.

Prefix means to place something before or in front.

Suffixes

Suffixes come after the root of a word.

Example: Feminism

Femin is a root. It means female, woman.

-ism means act, practice or process.

Feminism is the defining and establishing of equal political, economic, and social rights for women.

Unlike prefixes, **suffixes** can be used to change a word's part of speech.

Example: "Randy raced to the finish line." VS "Shana's costume was very racy."

In the first sentence, raced is a verb. In the second sentence, racy is an adjective. By changing the suffix from **-ed** to **-y**, the word race changes from a verb into an adjective, which has an entirely different meaning.

Although you cannot determine the meaning of a word by a prefix or suffix alone, you *can* use your knowledge of what root words mean to eliminate answer choices; indicating if the word is positive or negative can give you a partial meaning of the word.

Study Tips for Improving Vocabulary and Grammar

1. You're probably pretty computer savvy and know the Internet very well. Visit the Online Writing Lab website, which is sponsored by Purdue University, at http://owl.english.purdue.edu. This site provides you with an excellent overview of syntax, writing style, and strategy. It also has helpful and lengthy review sections that include multiple-choice "Test Your Knowledge" quizzes, which provide immediate answers to the questions.

2. It's beneficial to read the entire passage first to determine its intended meaning BEFORE you attempt to answer any questions. Doing so provides you with key insight into a passage's syntax (especially verb tense, subject-verb agreement, modifier placement, writing style, and punctuation).

3. When you answer a question, use the "Process-of-Elimination Method" to determine the best answer. Try each of the four answers and determine which one BEST fits with the meaning of the paragraph. Find the BEST answer. Chances are that the BEST answer is the CORRECT answer.

Test Your Knowledge: Writing

1. "The medication must be properly administered to the patient."
   Which of the words in the above sentence is an adverb?
   - a) Medication.
   - b) Properly.
   - c) Administered.
   - d) Patient.

2. "The old man had trouble walking if he did not have his walker and had a long way to go."
   What is the subject of the sentence?
   - a) Walker.
   - b) His.
   - c) Trouble.
   - d) Man.

3. "The boy decided ___ would ride his bike now that the sun was shining."
   Which of the following pronouns completes the sentence?
   - a) His.
   - b) Him.
   - c) He.
   - d) They.

4. "The impatient student hurried through the test and failed as a result."
   Which word is an adjective?
   - a) Hurried.
   - b) Result.
   - c) Impatient.
   - d) Student.

5. Correct the verb: "The nurse decided it were a good time to follow up with a patient about their medication."
   - a) Was.
   - b) Is.
   - c) Has.
   - d) No error.

Use context clues to determine the meaning of each underlined word.

6. His story didn't seem very realistic; even though it was a documentary.
   - a) Believable.
   - b) Humorous.
   - c) Poetic.
   - d) Exciting.

7. Listening to music too loudly, especially through headphones, can <u>impair</u> your hearing.
    a) Damage.
    b) Heighten.
    c) Use.
    d) Ensure.

8. Kelly's game happened to <u>coincide</u> with the Sue's recital.
    a) Happen before.
    b) Occur at the same time.
    c) Occur afterward.
    d) Not happen.

9. The weather has been very extreme lately; thankfully, today it's much more <u>temperate</u>.
    a) Troubling.
    b) Beautiful.
    c) Cold.
    d) Moderate.

10. He knew he couldn't win the race after falling off his bike, so he had to <u>concede</u>.
    a) Continue.
    b) Give up.
    c) Challenge.
    d) Be thankful.

11. The editor, preferring a more <u>terse</u> writing style, cut 30% of the words from the article.
    a) Elegant.
    b) Factual.
    c) Descriptive.
    d) Concise.

12. Victor Frankenstein spent the last years of his life chasing his <u>elusive</u> monster, which was always one step ahead.
    a) Unable to be compared.
    b) Unable to be captured.
    c) Unable to be forgotten.
    d) Unable to be avoided.

13. Certain <u>passages</u> were taken from the book for the purpose of illustration.
    a) Excerpts.
    b) Contents.
    c) Paragraphs.
    d) Tables.

14. The investigator searched among the <u>ruins</u> for the cause of the fire.
    a) Terminal.
    b) Foundation.
    c) Rubble.
    d) Establishment.

15. To make her novels more engaging, Cynthia was known to <u>embellish</u> her writing with fictitious details.
- a) Add to.
- b) Detract.
- c) Isolate.
- d) Disavow.

16. Robert's well-timed joke served to <u>diffuse</u> the tension in the room and the party continued happily.
- a) Refuse.
- b) Intensify.
- c) Create.
- d) Soften.

17. I had a difficult time understanding the book because the author kept <u>digressing</u> to unrelated topics.
- a) Deviating, straying.
- b) Regressing, reverting.
- c) Changing the tone.
- d) Expressing concisely.

18. The senator <u>evaded</u> almost every question.
- a) Avoided.
- b) Answered indirectly.
- c) Refused to answer directly.
- d) Deceived.

19. Sammie hasn't come out of her room all afternoon, but I would <u>surmise</u> that it is because she is upset about not being able to go to the mall.
- a) Confirm.
- b) Surprise.
- c) Believe.
- d) Guess.

20. The details can be worked out later; what's important is that the company follows the <u>crux</u> of the argument, which is that everyone be paid equally.
- a) Overall tone.
- b) Specific fact.
- c) Main point.
- d) Logic, reasoning.

Use context clues to choose the best word to complete the sentence.

21. Mr. Collins _____ tomatoes so vehemently that he felt ill just smelling them.
- a) Resented
- b) Disliked
- c) Detested
- d) Hated

22. We were rolling on the ground with laughter during the _____ new movie.
    a) Comical
    b) Humorous
    c) Amusing
    d) Hilarious

23. Tina's parents made us feel right at home during our visit to their house with their generous _____.
    a) Unselfishness
    b) Politeness
    c) Hospitality
    d) Charity

24. Although his mother was not happy that he broke the window, she was pleased that he was _____ about it.
    a) Honest
    b) Trustworthy
    c) Authentic
    d) Decent

25. The soldiers _____ to their feet immediately when then officer walked into the room.
    a) Stood
    b) Leapt
    c) Rose
    d) Skipped

Test Your Knowledge: Writing – Answers

1. **b)**
"Properly" is the adverb which describes the verb "administered."

2. **d)**
Although there are other nouns in the sentence, the "man" is the subject.

3. **c)**
"He" is the correct answer; the other pronouns are possessive or otherwise in the wrong tense.

4. **c)**
"Impatient" describes the noun "student."

5. **a)**
"Was" is the correct answer; the other choices are in the wrong tense.

6. **a) Believable.**
Realistic means accurate, truthful, and believable.

7. **a) Damage.**
This is the only logical choice.

8. **b) Occur at the same time.**
According to information in the sentence, the game was scheduled at the same time as the recital.

9. **d) Moderate.**
The context says that the weather has been "extreme." It does not say if the weather has been extremely hot or cold; therefore, choices **b) Beautiful** and **c) Cold** can be ruled out. The sentence also indicates a change from negative to positive making moderate the best choice.

10. **b) Give up.**
The speaker of the sentence knows they cannot win, so choice **b)** is the best choice.

11. **d) Concise.**
Terse means concise, using no unnecessary words. The main clue is that the editor cut words from the article, reducing its wordiness.

12. **b) Unable to be captured.**
Elusive means evasive, difficult to capture.

13. **a) Excerpt.**
An excerpt is a passage or quote from a book, article, or other publication

14. **c) Rubble** is synonymous with ruin.

15. a) Add to.
To embellish is to add details to a story to make it more appealing.

16. d) Soften.
The clues *tension* and *continue happily* tell you that **d)** is the best choice

17. a) To deviate, stray.
To digress means to deviate; to stray from the main subject in writing or speaking.

18. a) To avoid.
To evade means to avoid by cleverness. The senator avoids answering the question by changing the subject.

19. d) Guess.
The speaker is guessing why Samantha is upset based on circumstances; she has not actually given a reason.

20. c) Main point.
Crux means the central or main point, especially of a problem. The main context clue is that the speaker isn't concerned with the details but is focused on getting agreement on the main point.

21. c) Detested.
The knowledge that Mr. Collins feels ill just smelling tomatoes suggests that his hatred for tomatoes is intense; therefore, the best choice will be the most negative. To **dislike** tomatoes – choice **b)** – is the most neutral word, so this choice can be ruled out. **Resented** is a word that generally applies to people or their actions, ruling out choice **a)**. Given the choice between **c)** and **d)**, the most negative is **c) Detested**.

22. d) Hilarious.
The movie must be extremely funny for the audience to have this sort of reaction, and, while all of the answer choices are synonyms for funny, the only one that means extremely funny is choice **d) Hilarious**.

23. c) Hospitality.
Although all four choices describe different types of kindness, **unselfishness** – choice **a)** – can be ruled out because it has the same basic meaning as the adjective, generous. Choice **d) Charity** is a kindness usually associated with those less fortunate; since nothing in the context indicates this type of relationship, this choice can also be eliminated.

Left with choices **b) Politeness** and **c) Hospitality**, hospitality best describes the kindness of welcoming someone into your home.

24. a) Honest.
Again we have a case in which all of the word choices are synonyms for the word honest. In this case, the most neutral word is the best choice. Choice **b) Trustworthy**, **c) Authentic**, and **d) Decent** do not make as much sense as the most basic synonym, **honest**.

25. b) Leapt. The word immediately is the main clue. **a) Stood** and **c) Rose** are neutral words that do not convey a sense of urgency. Choice **b) Leapt** is the only word that implies the immediacy demanded by the sentence context.

Chapter 2: The Math Section

Before we begin our review, remember that there is no wrong-answer penalty on this exam, so try not to leave an answer selection blank. Of course, since the objective is to get as many right answers as possible, always use the process of elimination before choosing your answer. While the amount of time allotted for this section may seem like too little for the amount of questions, many of the questions are designed to be simpler than others.

The Most Common Mistakes

People make mistakes all the time – but during a test, those mistakes can cost you a passing score. Watch out for these common mistakes that people make on the PARAPRO:

- Answering with the wrong sign (positive / negative).

- Mixing up the Order of Operations.

- Misplacing a decimal.

- Not reading the question thoroughly (and therefore providing an answer that was not asked for.)

- Circling the wrong letter, or filling in wrong circle choice.

If you're thinking, "Those ideas are just common sense" – exactly! Most of the mistakes made on the PARAPRO are simple mistakes. Regardless, they still result in a wrong answer and the loss of a potential point.

Helpful Strategies

1. **Go Back to the Basics**: First and foremost, practice your basic skills: sign changes, order of operations, simplifying fractions, and equation manipulation. These are the skills used most on the test, though they are applied in different contexts. Remember that when it comes right down to it, all math problems rely on the four basic skills of addition, subtraction, multiplication, and division. All that changes is the order in which they are used to solve a problem.

2. **Don't Rely on Mental Math**: Using mental math is great for eliminating answer choices, but ALWAYS WRITE IT DOWN! This cannot be stressed enough. Use whatever paper is provided; by writing and/or drawing out the problem, you are more likely to catch any mistakes. The act of writing things down forces you to organize your calculations, leading to an improvement in your score.

3. **The Three-Times Rule**:

- **Step One – Read the question**: Write out the given information.

- **Step Two – Read the question**: Set up your equation(s) and solve.

- **Step Three – Read the question:** Make sure that your answer makes sense (is the amount too large or small, is the answer in the correct unit of measure, etc.).

4. **Make an Educated Guess**: Eliminate those answer choices which you are relatively sure are incorrect, and then guess from the remaining choices. Educated guessing is critical to increasing your score.

Calculators

No calculators! It is very important that you do not let yourself cheat while practicing. You will only be cheating yourself out of a better score on test day.

Math Concepts Tested on the ParaPro

You need to practice in order to score well on the test. To make the most out of your practice, use this guide to determine the areas for which you need more review. Most importantly, practice all areas under testing circumstances (a quiet area, a timed practice test, no looking up facts as you practice, etc.)

When reviewing, take your time and let your brain recall the necessary math. If you are taking this test, then you have already had course instruction in these areas. The examples given will "jog" your memory.

The next few pages will cover various math subjects (starting with the basics, but in no particular order), along with worked examples.

Order of Operations

PEMDAS – **P**arentheses/**E**xponents/**M**ultiply/**D**ivide/**A**dd/**S**ubtract

Perform the operations within parentheses first, and then any exponents. After those steps, perform all multiplication and division. (These are done from left to right, as they appear in the problem) Finally, do all required addition and subtraction, also from left to right as they appear in the problem.

Examples:

Solve $(-(2)^2 - (4 + 7))$.

$(-4 - 11) = -$ **15**.

Solve $((5)^2 \div 5 + 4 * 2)$.

$25 \div 5 + 4 * 2$.

$5 + 8 =$ **13**.

Positive & Negative Number Rules

$(+) + (-)$ = Subtract the two numbers. Solution gets the sign of the larger number.

$(-) + (-)$ = Negative number.

$(-) * (-)$ = Positive number.

$(-) * (+)$ = Negative number.

$(-) / (-)$ = Positive number.

$(-) / (+)$ = Negative number.

Fractions

Adding and subtracting fractions requires a common denominator.

Find a common denominator for:

$$\frac{2}{3} - \frac{1}{5}$$

$$\frac{2}{3} - \frac{1}{5} = \frac{2}{3}\left(\frac{5}{5}\right) - \frac{1}{5}\left(\frac{3}{3}\right) = \frac{10}{15} - \frac{3}{15} = \frac{7}{15}$$

To add mixed fractions, work first the whole numbers, and then the fractions.

$$2\frac{1}{4} + 1\frac{3}{4} = 3\frac{4}{4} = 4$$

To subtract mixed fractions, convert to single fractions by multiplying the whole number by the denominator and adding the numerator. Then work as above.

$$2\frac{1}{4} - 1\frac{3}{4} = \frac{9}{4} - \frac{7}{4} = \frac{2}{4} = \frac{1}{2}$$

To multiply fractions, convert any mixed fractions into single fractions and multiply across; reduce to lowest terms if needed.

$$2\frac{1}{4} * 1\frac{3}{4} = \frac{9}{4} * \frac{7}{4} = \frac{63}{16} = 3\frac{15}{16}$$

To divide fractions, convert any mixed fractions into single fractions, flip the second fraction, and then multiply across.

$$2\frac{1}{4} \div 1\frac{3}{4} = \frac{9}{4} \div \frac{7}{4} = \frac{9}{4} * \frac{4}{7} = \frac{36}{28} = 1\frac{8}{28} = 1\frac{2}{7}$$

Absolute Value

The absolute value of a number is its distance from zero, not its value.

So in $|x| = a$, "x" will equal "$-a$" as well as "a."

Likewise, $|\,3\,| = 3$, and $|-3\,| = 3$.

Equations with absolute values will have two answers. Solve each absolute value possibility separately. All solutions must be checked into the original equation.

Example: Solve for x:
$|2x - 3| = x + 1$.

Equation One: $2x - 3 = -(x + 1)$.
$2x - 3 = -x - 1$.
$3x = 2$.
$x = 2/3$.

Equation Two: $2x - 3 = x + 1$.
$x = 4$.

Simple Interest

Interest * Principle

Example: If I deposit $500 into an account with an annual rate of 5%, how much will I have after 2 years?

1st year: $500 + (500*.05) = 525$.

2nd year: $525 + (525*.05) = \mathbf{551.25}$.

26

Greatest Common Factor (GCF)

The greatest factor that divides two numbers.

Example: The GCF of 24 and 18 is 6. 6 is the largest number, or greatest factor, that can divide both 24 and 18.

Mean, Median, Mode

Mean is a math term for "average." Total all terms and divide by the number of terms.

Find the mean of 24, 27, and 18.

$24 + 27 + 18 = 69 \div 3 = $ **23**.

Median is the middle number of a given set, found after the numbers have all been put in numerical order. In the case of a set of even numbers, the middle two numbers are averaged.

What is the median of 24, 27, and 18?

18, **24**, 27.

What is the median of 24, 27, 18, and 19?

18, 19, 24, 27 ($19 + 24 = 43$. $43/2 = $ **21.5**).

Mode is the number which occurs most frequently within a given set.

What is the mode of 2, 5, 4, 4, 3, 2, 8, 9, 2, 7, 2, and 2?

The mode would be **2** because it appears the most within the set.

Percent, Part, & Whole

Part = Percent * Whole.

Percent = Part / Whole.

Whole = Part / Percent.

Example: Jim spent 30% of his paycheck at the fair. He spent $15 for a hat, $30 for a shirt, and $20 playing games. How much was his check? (Round to nearest dollar)

Whole = 65 / .30 = **$217.00**.

Percent Change

Percent Change = Amount of Change / Original Amount * 100.

Percent Increase = (New Amount – Original Amount) / Original Amount * 100.

Percent Decrease = (Original Amount – New Amount) / Original Amount * 100.

Amount Increase (or **Decrease**) = Original Price * Percent Markup (or Markdown).

Original Price = New Price / (Whole – Percent Markdown).

Original Price = New Price / (Whole + Percent Markup).

> **Example:** A car that was originally priced at $8300 has been reduced to $6995. What percent has it been reduced?
>
> (8300 – 6995) / 8300 * 100 = **15.72%**.

Repeated Percent Change

Increase: Final amount = Original Amount * $(1 + \text{Rate})^{\text{\# of changes}}$.

Decrease: Final Amount = Original Amount * $(1 - \text{Rate})^{\text{\# of changes}}$.

> **Example:** The weight of a tube of toothpaste decreases by 3% each time it is used. If it weighed 76.5 grams when new, what is its weight in grams after 15 uses?
>
> Final amount = $76.5 * (1 - .3)^{15}$.
>
> $76.5 * (.97)^{15}$ = **48.44 grams**.

Ratios

To solve a ratio, simply find the equivalent fraction. To distribute a whole across a ratio:

1. Total all parts.

2. Divide the whole by the total number of parts.

3. Multiply quotient by corresponding part of ratio.

> **Example:** There are 90 voters in a room, and they are either Democrat or Republican. The ratio of Democrats to Republicans is 5:4. How many Republicans are there?
>
> Step 1   5 + 4 = 9.
>
> Step 2   90 / 9 = 10.
>
> Step 3   10 * 4 = **40 Republicans**.

Proportions

Direct Proportions: Corresponding ratio parts change in the same direction (increase/decrease).

Indirect Proportions: Corresponding ratio parts change in opposite directions (as one part increases the other decreases).

Example: A train traveling 120 miles takes 3 hours to get to its destination. How long will it take if the train travels 180 miles?

120 mph:180 mph is to x hours:3 hours.

(Write as fraction and cross multiply.)

120/3 = 180/x.

540 = 120x.

x = **4.5 hours**.

Probabilities

A probability is found by dividing the number of desired outcomes by the number of possible outcomes. (The piece divided by the whole.)

Example: What is the probability of picking a blue marble if 3 of the 15 marbles are blue?

3/15 = 1/5. The probability is **1 in 5** that a blue marble is picked.

Math and Quantitative Reasoning Sequence

Each term is equal to the previous term plus x.

Example: 2, 5, 8, 11.

x = **3**.

2 + 3 = 5; 5 + 3 = 8 ... etc.

Geometric Sequence

Each term is equal to the previous term multiplied by x.

Example: 2, 4, 8, 16.

x = **2**.

Prime Factorization

Expand to prime number factors.

Example: $104 = 2 * 2 * 2 * 13$.

Exponent Rules

Rule	Example
$x^0 = 1$	$5^0 = 1$
$x^1 = x$	$5^1 = 5$
$x^a \cdot x^b = x^{a+b}$	$5^2 * 5^3 = 5^5$
$(xy)^a = x^a y^a$	$(5 * 6)^2 = 5^2 * 6^2 = 25 * 36$
$(x^a)^b = x^{ab}$	$(5^2)^3 = 5^6$
$(x/y)^a = x^a/y^a$	$(10/5)^2 = 10^2/5^2 = 100/25$
$x^a/y^b = x^{a-b}$	$5^4/5^3 = 5^1 = 5$ (remember $x \neq 0$)
$x^{1/a} = \sqrt[a]{x}$	$25^{1/2} = \sqrt[2]{25} = 5$
$x^{-a} = \dfrac{1}{x^a}$	$5^{-2} = \dfrac{1}{5^2} = \dfrac{1}{25}$ (remember $x \neq 0$)
$(-x)^a$ = positive number if "a" is even; negative number if "a" is odd.	

Roots

Root of a Product: $\sqrt[n]{a \cdot b} = \sqrt[n]{a} \cdot \sqrt[n]{b}$

Root of a Quotient: $\sqrt[n]{\dfrac{a}{b}} = \dfrac{\sqrt[n]{a}}{\sqrt[n]{b}}$

Fractional Exponent: $\sqrt[n]{a^m} = a^{m/n}$

Literal Equations

Equations with more than one variable. Solve in terms of one variable first.

Example: Solve for y: $4x + 3y = 3x + 2y$.

Step 1 – Combine like terms: $3y - 2y = 4x - 2x$.

Step 2 – Solve for y: $y = \mathbf{2x}$.

Slope

The formula used to calculate the slope (m) of a straight line connecting two points is: $m = (y_2 - y_1) / (x_2 - x_1)$ = change in y / change in x.

Example: Calculate slope of the line in the diagram:

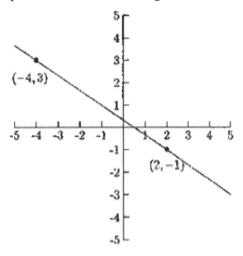

$m = (3 - (-1))/(-4 - 2) = 4/-6 = -2/3$.

Midpoint

To determine the midpoint between two points, simply add the two x coordinates together and divide by 2 (midpoint x). Then add the y coordinates together and divide by 2 (midpoint y).

$$\left(\frac{x_1 + x_2}{2}, \frac{y_1 + y}{2}\right)$$

Algebraic Equations

When simplifying or solving algebraic equations, you need to be able to utilize all math rules: exponents, roots, negatives, order of operations, etc.

1. Add & Subtract: Only the coefficients of like terms.

    Example: $5xy + 7y + 2yz + 11xy - 5yz = 16xy + 7y - 3yz$.

2. Multiplication: First the coefficients then the variables.

    Example: Monomial * Monomial.

    $(3x^4y^2z)(2y^4z^5) = 6x^4y^6z^6$.

    (A variable with no exponent has an implied exponent of 1.)

    Example: Monomial * Polynomial.

    $(2y^2)(y^3 + 2xy^2z + 4z) = 2y^5 + 4xy^4z + 8y^2z$.

31

Example: Binomial * Binomial.

$(5x + 2)(3x + 3)$.

(Remember FOIL – First, Outer, Inner, Last.)

First: $5x * 3x = 15x^2$.

Outer: $5x * 3 = 15x$.

Inner: $2 * 3x = 6x$.

Last: $2 * 3 = 6$.

Combine like terms: $15x^2 + 21x + 6$.

Example: Binomial * Polynomial.

$(x + 3)(2x^2 - 5x - 2)$.

First term: $x(2x^2 - 5x - 2) = 2x^3 - 5x^2 - 2x$.

Second term: $3(2x^2 - 5x - 2) = 6x^2 - 15x - 6$.

Added Together: $2x^3 + x^2 - 17x - 6$.

Inequalities

Inequalities are solved like linear and algebraic equations, except the sign must be reversed when dividing by a negative number.

Example: $-7x + 2 < 6 - 5x$.

Step 1 – Combine like terms: $-2x < 4$.

Step 2 – Solve for x. (Reverse the sign): $x > $ **-2.**

Solving compound inequalities will give you two answers.

Example: $-4 \leq 2x - 2 \leq 6$.

Step 1 – Add 2 to each term to isolate x: $-2 \leq 2x \leq 8$.

Step 2: Divide by 2: $-1 \leq x \leq 4$.

Solution set is **[-1, 4]**.

Fundamental Counting Principle

(The number of possibilities of an event happening) * (the number of possibilities of another event happening) = the total number of possibilities.

Example: If you take a multiple choice test with 5 questions, with 4 answer choices for each question, how many test result possibilities are there?

Solution: Question 1 has 4 choices; question 2 has 4 choices; etc.

4 *4 * 4 * 4 * 4 (one for each question) = **1024 possible test results**.

Permutations

The number of ways a set number of items can be arranged. Recognized by the use of a factorial (n!), with n being the number of items.

If n = 3, then 3! = 3 * 2 * 1 = 6. If you need to arrange n number of things but x number are alike, then n! is divided by x!

Example: How many different ways can the letters in the word **balance** be arranged?

Solution: There are 7 letters so $n! = 7!$ and 2 letters are the same so $x! = 2!$ Set up the equation:

$$\frac{7*6*5*4*3*2*1}{2*1} = \textbf{2540 ways}.$$

Combinations

To calculate total number of possible combinations use the formula:
n!/r! (n-r)!   n = # of objects   r = # of objects selected at a time

Example: If seven people are selected in groups of three, how many different combinations are possible?

Solution:

$$\frac{7*6*5*4*3*2*1}{(3*2*1)(7-3)} = \textbf{210 possible combinations}.$$

Geometry

- **Acute Angle**: Measures less than 90°.

- **Acute Triangle**: Each angle measures less than 90°.

- **Obtuse Angle**: Measures greater than 90°.

- **Obtuse Triangle**: One angle measures greater than 90°.

- **Adjacent Angles**: Share a side and a vertex.

- **Complementary Angles**: Adjacent angles that sum to 90°.

- **Supplementary Angles**: Adjacent angles that sum to 180°.

- **Vertical Angles**: Angles that are opposite of each other. They are always congruent (equal in measure).

- **Equilateral Triangle**: All angles are equal.

- **Isosceles Triangle**: Two sides and two angles are equal.

- **Scalene**: No equal angles.

- **Parallel Lines**: Lines that will never intersect. Y **ll** X means line Y is parallel to line X.

- **Perpendicular lines**: Lines that intersect or cross to form 90° angles.

- **Transversal Line**: A line that crosses parallel lines.

- **Bisector**: Any line that cuts a line segment, angle, or polygon exactly in half.
- **Polygon**: Any enclosed plane shape with three or more connecting sides (ex. a triangle).

- **Regular Polygon**: Has all equal sides and equal angles (ex. square).

- **Arc**: A portion of a circle's edge.

- **Chord**: A line segment that connects two different points on a circle.

- **Tangent**: Something that touches a circle at only one point without crossing through it.

- **Sum of Angles**: The sum of angles of a polygon can be calculated using $(n-1)180^\circ$, when n = the number of sides

Regular Polygons

Polygon Angle Principle: S = The sum of interior angles of a polygon with n-sides.

$S = (n - 2)180$.

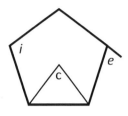

The measure of each central angle (c) is $360°/n$.
The measure of each interior angle (i) is $(n - 2)180°/n$.
The measure of each exterior angle (e) is $360°/n$.

To compare areas of similar polygons: $A_1/A_2 = (side_1/side_2)^2$.

Triangles

The angles in a triangle add up to $180°$.

Area of a triangle = $½ * b * h$, or $½bh$.

Pythagoras' Theorem: $a^2 + b^2 = c^2$.

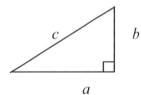

Trapezoids

Four-sided polygon, in which the bases (and only the bases) are parallel.
Isosceles Trapezoid – base angles are congruent.

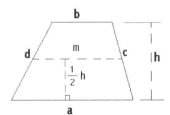

Area and Perimeter of a Trapezoid

$$m = \frac{1}{2}(a + b)$$

$$Area = \frac{1}{2} h * (a + b) = m * h$$

$$Perimeter = a + b + c + d = 2m + c + d$$

If m is the median then: $m \parallel \overline{AB}$ and $m \parallel CD$

35

Rhombus

Four-sided polygon, in which all four sides are congruent and opposite sides are parallel.

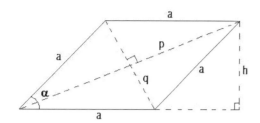

Area and Perimeter of a Rhombus

$$Perimeter = 4a$$

$$Area = a^2 \sin\alpha = a * h = \frac{1}{2}pq$$

$$4a^2 = p^2 + q^2$$

Rectangle

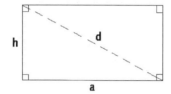

Area and Perimeter of a Rectangle

$$d = \sqrt{a^2 + h^2}$$

$$a = \sqrt{d^2 - h^2}$$

$$h = \sqrt{d^2 - a^2}$$

$$Perimeter = 2a + 2h$$

$$Area = a \cdot h$$

Square

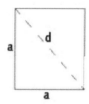

Area and Perimeter of a Square

$$d = a\sqrt{2}$$

$$Perimeter = 4a = 2d\sqrt{2}$$

$$Area = a^2 = \frac{1}{2}d^2$$

Circle

Area and Perimeter of a Circle

$$d = 2r$$

$$Perimeter = 2\pi r = \pi d$$

$$Area = \pi r^2$$

Cube

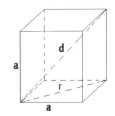

Area and Volume of a Cube

$r = a\sqrt{2}$

$d = a\sqrt{3}$

$Area = 6a^2$

$Volume = a^3$

Cuboid

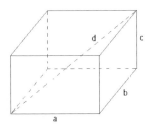

Area and Volume of a Cuboid

$d = \sqrt{a^2 + b^2 + c^2}$

$A = 2(ab + ac + bc)$

$V = abc$

Area and Volume of a Pyramid

$A_{lateral} = a\sqrt{h^2 + \left(\frac{b}{2}\right)^2} + b\sqrt{h^2 + \left(\frac{a}{2}\right)^2}$

$d = \sqrt{a^2 + b^2}$

$A_{base} = ab$

$A_{total} = A_{lateral} + A_{base}$

$V = \frac{1}{3}abh$

Test Your Knowledge: The Math Section

1. $3 * (2 * 4^3) \div 4 = ?$

2. $(4^3 + 2 - 1) = ?$

3. $(5 * 3) * 1 + 5 = ?$

4. $(7^2 - 2^3 - 6) = ?$

5. $(5^3 + 7) * 2 = ?$

6. If Lynn can type a page in p minutes, how many pages can she do in 5 minutes?
    a) $5/p$.
    b) $p - 5$.
    c) $p + 5$.
    d) $p/5$.
    e) $1 - p + 5$.

7. If Sally can paint a house in 4 hours, and John can paint the same house in 6 hours, how long will it take for both of them to paint the house together?
    a) 2 hours and 24 minutes.
    b) 3 hours and 12 minutes.
    c) 3 hours and 44 minutes.
    d) 4 hours and 10 minutes.
    e) 4 hours and 33 minutes.

8. The sales price of a car is $12,590, which is 20% off the original price. What is the original price?
    a) $14,310.40.
    b) $14,990.90.
    c) $15,290.70.
    d) $15,737.50.
    e) $16,935.80.

9. Solve the following equation for "A": $2A \div 3 = 8 + 4A$.
    a) -2.4.
    b) 2.4.
    c) 1.3.
    d) -1.3.
    e) 0.

10. If $y = 3$, then what is $y^3(y^3 - y)$?
    a) 300.
    b) 459.
    c) 648.
    d) 999.
    e) 1099.

11. Round 907.457 to the nearest tens place.
- a) 908.0.
- b) 910.
- c) 907.5.
- d) 900.
- e) 907.46

12. What is 1230.932567 rounded to the nearest hundredths place?
- a) 1200.
- b) 1230.9326.
- c) 1230.93.
- d) 1230.
- e) 1230.933.

13. Subtract the following numbers (First minus second minus third), and round to the nearest tenths place:

134.679
45.548
67.8807

- a) 21.3.
- b) 21.25.
- c) –58.97.
- d) –59.0.
- e) 1.

14. What is the absolute value of –9?
- a) –9.
- b) 9.
- c) 0.
- d) –1.
- e) 1.

15. What is the median of the following list of numbers: 4, 5, 7, 9, 10, and 12?
- a) 6.
- b) 7.5.
- c) 7.8.
- d) 8.
- e) 9.

16. What is the mathematical average of the number of weeks in a year, seasons in a year, and the number of days in January?
- a) 36.
- b) 33.
- c) 32.
- d) 31.
- e) 29.

17. $0.98 + 45.102 + 32.3333 + 31 + 0.00009 = ?$
   a) 368.573.
   b) 210.536299.
   c) 109.41539.
   d) 99.9975.
   e) 80.8769543.

18. Find $0.12 \div 1$.
   a) 12.
   b) 1.2.
   c) .12.
   d) .012.
   e) .0012.

19. $(9 \div 3) * (8 \div 4) = ?$
   a) 1.
   b) 6.
   c) 72.
   d) 576.
   e) 752.

20. $6 * 0 * 5 = ?$
   a) 30.
   b) 11.
   c) 25.
   d) 0.
   e) 27.

21. $7.95 \div 1.5 = ?$
   a) 2.4
   b) 5.3
   c) 6.2
   d) 7.3
   e) 7.5

22. Describe the following sequence in mathematical terms: 144, 72, 36, 18, and 9.
   a) Descending arithmetic sequence.
   b) Ascending arithmetic sequence.
   c) Descending geometric sequence.
   d) Ascending geometric sequence.
   e) Miscellaneous sequence.

23. Which of the following is not a whole number followed by its square?
   a) 1, 1.
   b) 6, 36.
   c) 8, 64.
   d) 10, 100.
   e) 11, 144.

24. There are 12 more apples than oranges in a basket of 36 apples and oranges. How many apples are in the basket?
  a) 12.
  b) 15.
  c) 24.
  d) 28.
  e) 36.

25. Which of the following correctly identifies 4 consecutive odd integers, where the sum of the middle two integers is equal to 24?
  a) 5, 7, 9, 11.
  b) 7, 9, 11, 13.
  c) 9, 11, 13, 15.
  d) 11, 13, 15, 17.
  e) 13, 15, 17, 19.

26. What is the next number in the sequence? 6, 12, 24, 48, ___.
  a) 72.
  b) 96.
  c) 108.
  d) 112.
  e) 124.

27. If the perimeter of a rectangular house is 44 yards, and the length is 36 feet, what is the width of the house?
  a) 30 feet.
  b) 18 yards.
  c) 28 feet.
  d) 32 feet.
  e) 36 yards.

28. What is the volume of a cylinder with a diameter of 1 foot and a height of 14 inches?
  a) 2104.91 cubic inches.
  b) 1584 cubic inches.
  c) 528 cubic inches.
  d) 904.32 cubic inches.
  e) 264 cubic inches.

29. What is the volume of a cube whose width is 5 inches?
  a) 15 cubic inches.
  b) 25 cubic inches.
  c) 64 cubic inches.
  d) 100 cubic inches.
  e) 125 cubic inches.

30. A can's diameter is 3 inches, and its height is 8 inches. What is the volume of the can?
  a) 50.30 cubic inches.
  b) 56.57 cubic inches.
  c) 75.68 cubic inches.
  d) 113.04 cubic inches.
  e) 226.08 cubic inches.

31. If the area of a square flowerbed is 16 square feet, then how many feet is the perimeter of the flowerbed?
  a) 4.
  b) 12.
  c) 16.
  d) 20.
  e) 24.

32. If a discount of 25% off the retail price of a desk saves Mark $45, what was the original price of the desk?
  a) $135.
  b) $160.
  c) $180.
  d) $210.
  e) $215.

33. A customer pays $1,100 in state taxes on a newly-purchased car. What is the value of the car if state taxes are 8.9% of the value?
  a) $9.765.45
  b) $10,876.90
  c) $12,359.55
  d) $14,345.48
  e) $15,745.45

34. 35% of what number is 70?
  a) 100.
  b) 110.
  c) 150.
  d) 175.
  e) 200.

35. What number is 5% of 2000?
  a) 50.
  b) 100.
  c) 150.
  d) 200.
  e) 250.

Test Your Knowledge: The Math Section – Answers

1. 96.

2. 65.

3. 20.

4. 35.

5. 264.

6. a)

7. a)

8. d)

9. a)

10. c)

11. b)

12. c)

13. a)

14. b)

15. d)

16. e)

17. c)

18. c)

19. b)

20. d)

21. b)

22. c)

23. e)

24. c)

25. c)

26. b)

27. a)

28. b)

29. e)

30. b)

31. c)

32. c)

33. c)

34. e)

35. b)

Chapter 3: The Reading Section

The Reading section of the ParaPro Exam measures your ability to understand, analyze, and evaluate written passages. The passages will contain material from a variety of sources, and will cover a number of different topics.

There are many elements within the passages which you will be asked to identify and/or comprehend.

The Main Idea

Finding and understanding the main idea of a text is an essential reading skill. When you look past the facts and information and get to the heart of what the writer is trying to say, that's the **main idea**.

Imagine that you're at a friend's home for the evening:

> "Here," he says, "Let's watch this movie."

> "Sure," you reply. "What's it about?"

You'd like to know a little about what you'll be watching, but your question may not get you a satisfactory answer, because you've only asked about the subject of the film. The subject—what the movie is about—is only half the story. Think, for example, about all the alien invasion films ever been made. While these films may share the same general subject, what they have to say about the aliens or about humanity's theoretical response to invasion may be very different. Each film has different ideas it wants to convey about a subject, just as writers write because they have something they want to say about a particular subject. When you look beyond the facts and information to what the writer really wants to say about his or her subject, you're looking for the main idea.

One of the most common questions on reading comprehension exams is, "What is the main idea of this passage?" How would you answer this question for the paragraph below?

> "Wilma Rudolph, the crippled child who became an Olympic running champion, is an inspiration for us all. Born prematurely in 1940, Wilma spent her childhood battling illness, including measles, scarlet fever, chicken pox, pneumonia, and polio, a crippling disease which at that time had no cure. At the age of four, she was told she would never walk again. But Wilma and her family refused to give up. After years of special treatment and physical therapy, 12-year-old Wilma was able to walk normally again. But walking wasn't enough for Wilma, who was determined to be an athlete. Before long, her talent earned her a spot in the 1956 Olympics, where she earned a bronze medal. In the 1960 Olympics, the height of her career, she won three gold medals."

What is the main idea of this paragraph? You might be tempted to answer, "Wilma Rudolph" or "Wilma Rudolph's life." Yes, Wilma Rudolph's life is the **subject** of the passage—who or what the passage is about—but the subject is not necessarily the main idea. The **main idea** is what the writer wants to say about this subject. What is the main thing the writer says about Wilma's life?

Which of the following statements is the main idea of the paragraph?

a) Wilma Rudolph was very sick as a child.
b) Wilma Rudolph was an Olympic champion.
c) Wilma Rudolph is someone to admire.

Main idea: The overall fact, feeling, or thought a writer wants to convey about his or her subject.

The best answer is **c)**: Wilma Rudolph is someone to admire. This is the idea the paragraph adds up to; it's what holds all of the information in the paragraph together. This example also shows two important characteristics of a main idea:

1. It is **general** enough to encompass all of the ideas in the passage.

2. It is an **assertion.** An assertion is a statement made by the writer.

The main idea of a passage must be general enough to encompass all of the ideas in the passage. It should be broad enough for all of the other sentences in that passage to fit underneath it, like people under an umbrella. Notice that the first two options, "Wilma Rudolph was very sick as a child" and "Wilma Rudolph was an Olympic champion", are too specific to be the main idea. They aren't broad enough to cover all of the ideas in the passage, because the passage talks about both her illnesses and her Olympic achievements. Only the third answer is general enough to be the main idea of the paragraph.

A main idea is also some kind of **assertion** about the subject. An assertion is a claim that something is true. Assertions can be facts or opinions, but in either case, an assertion should be supported by specific ideas, facts, and details. In other words, the main idea makes a general assertion that tells readers that something is true.

The supporting sentences, on the other hand, show readers that this assertion is true by providing specific facts and details. For example, in the Wilma Rudolph paragraph, the writer makes a general assertion: "Wilma Rudolph, the crippled child who became an Olympic running champion, is an inspiration for us all." The other sentences offer specific facts and details that prove why Wilma Rudolph is an inspirational person.

Writers often state their main ideas in one or two sentences so that readers can have a very clear understanding about the main point of the passage. A sentence that expresses the main idea of a paragraph is called a **topic sentence.**

Notice, for example, how the first sentence in the Wilma Rudolph paragraph states the main idea:

"Wilma Rudolph, the crippled child who became an Olympic running champion, is an inspiration for us all."

This sentence is therefore the topic sentence for the paragraph. Topic sentences are often found at the beginning of paragraphs. Sometimes, though, writers begin with specific supporting ideas and lead up to the main idea, and in this case the topic sentence is often found at the end of the paragraph. Sometimes the topic sentence is even found somewhere in the middle, and other times there isn't a clear topic sentence at all—but that doesn't mean there isn't a main idea; the author has just chosen not to express it in a clear topic sentence. In this last case, you'll have to look carefully at the paragraph for clues about the main idea.

Main Ideas vs. Supporting Ideas

If you're not sure whether something is a main idea or a supporting idea, ask yourself the following question: is the sentence making a **general statement,** or is it providing **specific information?** In the Wilma Rudolph paragraph above, for example, all of the sentences except the first make specific statements. They are not general enough to serve as an umbrella or net for the whole paragraph.

Writers often provide clues that can help you distinguish between main ideas and their supporting ideas. Here are some of the most common words and phrases used to introduce specific examples:

1. **For example...**

2. **Specifically...**

3. **In addition...**

4. **Furthermore...**

5. **For instance...**

6. **Others...**

7. **In particular...**

8. **Some...**

These signal words tell you that a supporting fact or idea will follow. If you're having trouble finding the main idea of a paragraph, try eliminating sentences that begin with these phrases, because they will most likely be too specific to be a main ideas.

Implied Main Idea

When the main idea is **implied**, there's no topic sentence, which means that finding the main idea requires some detective work. But don't worry! You already know the importance of structure, word choice, style, and tone. Plus, you know how to read carefully to find clues, and you know that these clues will help you figure out the main idea.

For Example:

"One of my summer reading books was *The Windows of Time*. Though it's more than 100 pages long, I read it in one afternoon. I couldn't wait to see what happened to Evelyn, the main character. But by the time I got to the end, I wondered if I should have spent my afternoon doing something else. The ending was so awful that I completely forgot that I'd enjoyed most of the book."

There's no topic sentence here, but you should still be able to find the main idea. Look carefully at what the writer says and how she says it. What is she suggesting?

    a) *The Windows of Time* is a terrific novel.
    b) *The Windows of Time* is disappointing.
    c) *The Windows of Time* is full of suspense.
    d) *The Windows of Time* is a lousy novel.

The correct answer is **b)** – the novel is disappointing. How can you tell that this is the main idea? First, we can eliminate choice **c)**, because it's too specific to be a main idea. It deals only with one specific aspect of the novel (its suspense).

Sentences **a)**, **b)**, and **d)**, on the other hand, all express a larger idea – a general assertion about the quality of the novel. But only one of these statements can actually serve as a "net" for the whole paragraph. Notice that while the first few sentences praise the novel, the last two criticize it. Clearly, this is a mixed review.

Therefore, the best answer is **b)**. Sentence **a)** is too positive and doesn't account for the "awful" ending. Sentence **d)**, on the other hand, is too negative and doesn't account for the reader's sense of suspense and interest in the main character. But sentence **b)** allows for both positive and negative aspects – when a good thing turns bad, we often feel disappointed.

Now let's look at another example. Here, the word choice will be more important, so read carefully.

> "Fortunately, none of Toby's friends had ever seen the apartment where Toby lived with his mother and sister. Sandwiched between two burnt-out buildings, his two-story apartment building was by far the ugliest one on the block. It was a real eyesore: peeling orange paint (orange!), broken windows, crooked steps, crooked everything. He could just imagine what his friends would say if they ever saw this poor excuse for a building."

Which of the following expresses the main idea of this paragraph?

    a) Toby wishes he could move to a nicer building.
    b) Toby wishes his dad still lived with them.
    c) Toby is glad none of his friends know where he lives.
    d) Toby is sad because he doesn't have any friends.

From the description, we can safely assume that Toby doesn't like his apartment building and wishes he could move to a nicer building **a)**. But that idea isn't general enough to cover the whole paragraph, because it's about his building.

Because the first sentence states that Toby has friends, the answer cannot be **d)**. We know that Toby lives only with his mother and little sister, so we might assume that he wishes his dad still lived with them, **b)**, but there's nothing in the paragraph to support that assumption, and this idea doesn't include the two main topics of the paragraph—Toby's building and Toby's friends.

What the paragraph adds up to is that Toby is terribly embarrassed about his building, and he's glad that none of his friends have seen it **c)**. This is the main idea. The paragraph opens with the word "fortunately," so we know that he thinks it's a good thing none of his friends have been to his house. Plus, notice how the building is described: "by far the ugliest on the block," which says a lot since it's stuck "between two burnt-out buildings." The writer calls it an "eyesore," and repeats "orange" with an exclamation point to emphasize how ugly the color is. Everything is "crooked" in this "poor excuse for a building." Toby is clearly ashamed of where he lives and worries about what his friends would think if they saw it.

Cause and Effect

Understanding cause and effect is important for reading success. Every event has at least one cause (what made it happen) and at least one effect (the result of what happened). Some events have more than one cause, and some have more than one effect. An event is also often part of a chain of causes and effects. Causes and effects are usually signaled by important transitional words and phrases.

Words Indicating Cause:

1. **Because (of)**

2. **Created (by)**

3. **Caused (by)**

4. **Since**

Words Indicating Effect:

1. **As a result**

2. **Since**

3. **Consequently**

4. **So**

5. **Hence**

6. **Therefore**

Sometimes, a writer will offer his or her opinion about why an event happened when the facts of the cause(s) aren't clear. Or a writer may predict what he or she thinks will happen because of a certain event (its effects). If this is the case, you need to consider how reasonable those opinions are. Are the writer's ideas logical? Does the writer offer support for the conclusions he or she offers?

Reading Between the Lines

Paying attention to word choice is particularly important when the main idea of a passage isn't clear. A writer's word choice doesn't just affect meaning; it also creates it. For example, look at the following description from a teacher's evaluation of a student applying to a special foreign language summer camp.

There's no topic sentence, but if you use your powers of observation, you should be able to tell how the writer feels about her subject.

> "As a student, Jane usually completes her work on time and checks it carefully. She speaks French well and is learning to speak with less of an American accent. She has often been a big help to other students who are just beginning to learn the language."

What message does this passage send about Jane? Is she the best French student the writer has ever had? Is she one of the worst, or is she just average? To answer these questions, you have to make an inference, and you must support your inference with specific observations. What makes you come to the conclusion that you come to?

The **diction** of the paragraph above reveals that this is a positive evaluation, but not a glowing recommendation.

Here are some of the specific observations you might have made to support this conclusion:

- The writer uses the word "usually" in the first sentence. This means that Jane is good about meeting deadlines for work, but not great; she doesn't always hand in her work on time.

- The first sentence also says that Jane checks her work carefully. While Jane may sometimes hand in work late, at least she always makes sure it's quality work. She's not sloppy.

- The second sentence tells us she's "learning to speak with less of an American accent." This suggests that she has a strong accent and needs to improve in this area. It also suggests, though, that she is already making progress.

- The third sentence tells us that she "often" helps "students who are just beginning to learn the language." From this we can conclude that Jane has indeed mastered the basics. Otherwise, how could she be a big help to students who are just starting to learn? By looking at the passage carefully, then, you can see how the writer feels about her subject.

Test Your Knowledge: The Reading Section

Read each of the following paragraphs carefully and answer the questions that follow.

My "office" measures a whopping 5 x 7 feet. A large desk is squeezed into one corner, leaving just enough room for a rickety chair between the desk and the wall. Yellow paint is peeling off the walls in dirty chunks. The ceiling is barely six feet tall; it's like a hat that I wear all day long. The window, a single 2 x 2 pane, looks out onto a solid brick wall just two feet away.

1. What is the main idea implied by this paragraph?
    a) This office is small but comfortable.
    b) This office is in need of repair.
    c) This office is old and claustrophobic.
    d) None of the above.

There are many things you can do to make tax time easier. The single most important strategy is to keep accurate records. Keep all of your pay stubs, receipts, bank statements, and other relevant financial information in a neat, organized folder so that when you're ready to prepare your form, all of your paperwork is in one place. The second thing you can do is start early. Get your tax forms from the post office as soon as they are available and start calculating. This way, if you run into any problems, you have plenty of time to straighten them out. You can also save time by reading the directions carefully. This will prevent time-consuming errors. Finally, if your taxes are relatively simple (you don't have itemized deductions or special investments), use the shorter tax form. It's only one page, so if your records are in order, it can be completed in less than an hour.

2. How many suggestions for tax time does this passage offer?
    a) One.
    b) Two.
    c) Three.
    d) Four.

3. The sentence "It's only one page, so if your records are in order, it can be completed in less than an hour" is:
    a) The main idea of the passage.
    b) A major supporting idea.
    c) A minor supporting idea.
    d) A transitional sentence.

4. A good summary of this passage would be:
    a) Simple strategies can make tax time less taxing.
    b) Don't procrastinate at tax time.
    c) Always keep good records.
    d) Get a tax attorney.

5. According to the passage, who should use the shorter tax form?
    a) Everybody.
    b) People who do not have complicated finances.
    c) People who do have complicated finances.
    d) People who wait until the last minute to file taxes.

6. The sentence, "The single most important strategy is to keep accurate records," is a(n):
  a) Fact.
  b) Opinion.
  c) Both of the above.
  d) Neither of the above.

Being a secretary is a lot like being a parent. After a while, your boss becomes dependent upon you, just as a child is dependent upon his or her parents. Like a child who must ask permission before going out, you'll find your boss coming to you for permission, too. "Can I have a meeting on Tuesday at 3:30?" you might be asked, because you're the one who keeps track of your boss's schedule. You will also find yourself cleaning up after your boss a lot, tidying up papers and files the same way a parent tucks away a child's toys and clothes. And, like a parent protects his or her children from outside dangers, you will find yourself protecting your boss from certain "dangers"—unwanted callers, angry clients, and upset subordinates.

7. The main idea of this passage is:
  a) Secretaries are treated like children.
  b) Bosses treat their secretaries like children.
  c) Secretaries and parents have similar roles.
  d) Bosses depend too much upon their secretaries.

8. Which of the following is the topic sentence of the paragraph?
  a) Being a secretary is a lot like being a parent.
  b) After a while, your boss becomes dependent upon you, just as a child is dependent upon his or her parents.
  c) You will also find yourself cleaning up after your boss a lot, tidying up papers and files the same way a parent tucks away a child's toys and clothes.
  d) None of the above.

9. According to the passage, secretaries are like parents in which of the following ways?
  a) They make their bosses' lives possible.
  b) They keep their bosses from things that might harm or bother them.
  c) They're always cleaning and scrubbing things.
  d) They don't get enough respect.

10. This passage uses which point of view?
  a) First person.
  b) Second person.
  c) Third person.
  d) First and second person.

11. The tone of this passage suggests that:
  a) The writer is angry about how secretaries are treated.
  b) The writer thinks secretaries do too much work.
  c) The writer is slightly amused by how similar the roles of secretaries and parents are.
  d) The writer is both a secretary and a parent.

12. The sentence, "'Can't I have a meeting on Tuesday at 3:30?' you might be asked, because you're the one who keeps track of your boss's schedule," is a:
   a) Main idea.
   b) Major supporting idea.
   c) Minor supporting idea
   d) None of the above.

13. "Being a secretary is a lot like being a parent" is:
   a) A fact.
   b) An opinion.
   c) Neither of the above.
   d) Both of the above.

14. The word "subordinates" probably means:
   a) Employees.
   b) Parents.
   c) Clients.
   d) Secretaries.

Day after day, Johnny chooses to sit at his computer instead of going outside with his friends. A few months ago, he'd get half a dozen phone calls from his friends every night. Now, he might get one or two a week. It used to be that his friends would come over two or three days a week after school. Now, he spends his afternoons alone with his computer.

15. The main idea is:
   a) Johnny and his friends are all spending time with their computers instead of one another.
   b) Johnny's friends aren't very good friends.
   c) Johnny has alienated his friends by spending so much time on the computer.
   d) Johnny and his friends prefer to communicate by computer.

We've had Ginger since I was two years old. Every morning, she wakes me up by licking my cheek. That's her way of telling me she's hungry. When she wants attention, she'll weave in and out of my legs and meow until I pick her up and hold her. And I can always tell when Ginger wants to play. She'll bring me her toys and will keep dropping them (usually right on my homework!) until I stop what I'm doing and play with her for a while.

16. A good topic sentence for this paragraph would be:
   a) I take excellent care of Ginger.
   b) Ginger is a demanding pet.
   c) Ginger and I have grown up together.
   d) Ginger is good at telling me what she wants.

Test Your Knowledge: The Reading Section – Answers

1. c)

2. d)

3. c)

4. a)

5. b)

6. b)

7. c)

8. a)

9. b)

10. b)

11. c)

12. c)

13. b)

14. a)

15. c)

16. d)

Final Thoughts

In the end, we know that you will be successful in taking the ParaPro. Although the road ahead may at times be challenging, if you continue your hard work and dedication (just like you are doing to prepare right now!), you will find that your efforts will pay off.

If you are struggling after reading this book and following our guidelines, we sincerely hope that you will take note of our advice and seek additional help. Start by asking friends about the resources that they are using. If you are still not reaching the score you want, consider getting the help of a tutor.

If you are on a budget and cannot afford a private tutoring service, there are plenty of independent tutors, including college students who are proficient in the tested subjects. You don't have to spend thousands of dollars to afford a good tutor or review course.

We wish you the best of luck and happy studying. Most importantly, we hope you enjoy your coming years – after all, you put a lot of work into getting there in the first place.

Sincerely,
The Trivium Team

Made in the USA
Lexington, KY
07 February 2014